SportsZone Biographies

TOM BRADY

BY LUKE HANLON

SportsZone

An Imprint of Abdo Publishing

abdobooks.com

abdobooks.com

Published by Abdo Publishing, a division of ABDO, PO Box 398166, Minneapolis, Minnesota 55439.

Printed in the United States of America, North Mankato, Minnesota.
052023
092023

THIS BOOK CONTAINS RECYCLED MATERIALS

Cover Photo: Joe Robbins/AP Images
Interior Photos: Ben Liebenberg/AP Images, 5; Steve Luciano/AP Images, 6; Scott Audette/AP Images, 8; Al Messerschmidt Archive/AP Images, 11, 13; Greg Trott/AP Images, 14; Michael Hickey/Getty Images Sport/Getty Images, 17; Bob Leverone/Sporting News Archive/Sporting News/Getty Images, 18; Rob Tringali/SportsChrome/Getty Images, 21; Elise Amendola/AP Images, 23; Rob Carr/Getty Images Sport/Getty Images, 25; Maddie Meyer/Getty Images Sport/Getty Images, 27; Patrick Smith/Getty Images Sport/Getty Images, 29

Editors: Steph Giedd and Charlie Beattie
Series Designer: Karli Kruse

LIBRARY OF CONGRESS CONTROL NUMBER: 2022949108

Publisher's Cataloging-in-Publication Data

Names: Hanlon, Luke, author.
Title: Tom Brady / by Luke Hanlon
Description: Minneapolis, Minnesota: Abdo Publishing Company, 2024 | Series: SportsZone biographies | Includes online resources and index.
Identifiers: ISBN 9781098291723 (lib. bdg.) | ISBN 9781098278274 (ebook)
Subjects: LCSH: Brady, Tom, 1977--Juvenile literature. | Football players--Biography --Juvenile literature. | Quarterbacks (Football)--Biography--Juvenile literature. | Professional athletes—Biography--Juvenile literature.
Classification: DDC 796.092--dc23

TABLE OF CONTENTS

Chapter One

BRADY TAKES THE FIELD

Tom Brady lined up his Tampa Bay Buccaneers offense at the Kansas City Chiefs' 8-yard line. It was late in the first quarter of Super Bowl LV in February 2021, and Tampa Bay was down 3–0. But Brady had marched the Buccaneers down the field.

Brady took the snap in the shotgun formation. He faked a handoff to running back Leonard Fournette to fool Kansas City's defense into thinking it would be a running play. Meanwhile, Buccaneers tight end Rob Gronkowski broke from right to left across the field behind the offensive linemen. Brady lobbed a short toss to "Gronk." The big tight end turned upfield and cruised into the end zone to give the Buccaneers the lead.

The connection was something National Football League (NFL) fans were used to, especially in the playoffs.

Tampa Bay Buccaneers quarterback Tom Brady takes the field to start Super Bowl LV in 2021.

The dynamic duo of Brady, *right*, and Rob Gronkowski, *left*, celebrate their Super Bowl LV victory over the Kansas City Chiefs.

It was the 13th touchdown pass Brady had thrown to Gronkowski in a postseason game. That was the most between a quarterback and receiver in NFL history. But the previous 12 had come when the two played for the New England Patriots.

Brady was playing in his 21st NFL season in 2020. His first 20 were with the Patriots. But after the 2019 season, Brady couldn't agree to a contract extension with New England. He decided to sign with Tampa Bay. A year earlier, Gronkowski had announced his retirement from the NFL. Shortly after Brady signed with the

Buccaneers, he helped to convince his favorite target to join him in Tampa Bay.

The duo wasn't done in Super Bowl LV, though. With just over six minutes left in the second quarter, they connected again. Brady threw a 17-yard laser to Gronkowski in the back of the end zone. That put the Buccaneers up 14–3.

Brady threw a third touchdown before the first half was over. The Buccaneers went on to win 31–9. Brady was named the Most Valuable Player (MVP) of the Super Bowl. It was the seventh time he had hoisted the Vince Lombardi Trophy, awarded to the team who wins the Super Bowl. No other player had won more than five.

HUMBLE BEGINNINGS

Heading into college, Brady was not on track to be the greatest quarterback of all time. Most top college programs didn't recruit him while he was in high school in San Mateo, California. Brady's dad sent out highlight tapes to more than 50 schools in an effort to convince someone to give his son a scholarship. The University of Michigan took notice. Brady left for Michigan in

FAST FACT

Tom Brady excelled at both football and baseball in high school. Some of his high school teammates thought he would eventually play professional baseball. Brady was even drafted by the Montreal Expos in 1995.

the fall of 1996, but it took a while for him to play. There were six quarterbacks ahead of him on the depth chart. Brady finally became the starter in 1998. After watching Brady put up unspectacular numbers, Michigan coach Lloyd Carr tried

In Brady's final season at Michigan, he led the team to victory in the Orange Bowl and the No. 5 ranking in the country.

something different in 1999. After Brady, now a senior, started each game, sophomore Drew Henson would play the second quarter. The quarterback who played better would finish the game from there.

Brady played well enough to win the full-time starting job midway through the season. He helped lead Michigan on a five-game win streak to end his senior year. That included comeback victories over ranked opponents Penn State University and the University of Alabama.

FAST FACT

Because multiple quarterbacks in the 2000 NFL Draft were picked ahead of Brady, he thought he might not have a future in the NFL. After he finally heard his name called, Brady later said, "I was so excited. I don't have to be an insurance salesman, you know?" That was the career he would have pursued had he not been drafted.

Even that strong finish wasn't enough to impress NFL teams. Six quarterbacks were taken before Brady in the 2000 NFL Draft. The Patriots finally selected him with the 199th pick. Brady's skills were greatly underestimated, and he set out to prove wrong every team that had passed him over.

Chapter Two

UNLIKELY HERO

It can take time for rookie quarterbacks to see the field. That's especially true for quarterbacks taken late in the draft. In fact, many never see the field at all. Tom Brady didn't see much action in his rookie year, but eventually he earned the backup job going into the 2001 season.

The New England Patriots weren't counting on Brady at all. New England already had a successful starter in Drew Bledsoe. He had made three Pro Bowls and led the Patriots to a Super Bowl appearance in 1997. Entering the 2001 season, he was still considered one of the NFL's top quarterbacks.

Everything changed, though, on September 23, 2001. Late in the fourth quarter of a game against the New York Jets, Bledsoe tried to run for a first down. A Jets linebacker hit him hard near the sideline. Bledsoe was seriously injured by the hit, and Brady came on with 2:16 left in the game. The young quarterback marched the Patriots down the field to

Tom Brady earned his first Pro Bowl selection during his breakout 2001 season with the New England Patriots.

FAST FACT

Tom Brady's legendary confidence was on display even before he played a single down in the NFL. After being drafted by the Patriots, he happened to run into team owner Robert Kraft. According to Kraft, Brady smiled and said to the owner, "I'm the best decision this organization has ever made."

give them a chance to win. But they couldn't score a touchdown and lost 10–3.

The next week Brady started his first game against Peyton Manning and the Indianapolis Colts. Brady led the Pats to a 44–13 blowout win. It was the first of many quarterback duels between Brady and Manning.

Bledsoe eventually returned to full health. But Patriots head coach Bill Belichick decided to stick with Brady. The young quarterback had not put up spectacular numbers. But New England was winning. The Patriots ended the season on a six-game winning streak.

The streak continued into the conference championship game against the Pittsburgh Steelers. But Brady was injured in the second quarter. Bledsoe finished the game and threw the only touchdown pass of the day. New England won 24–17 to clinch a spot in Super Bowl XXXVI. New England was up against the St. Louis Rams. The Rams led the NFL in scoring that season, averaging more than 31 points per game. That earned them the nickname "The Greatest Show on Turf." Most people thought St. Louis would win easily. But Brady and the Patriots weren't fazed.

Injured quarterback Drew Bledsoe, *left*, talks strategy with Brady during an October 2001 game.

They led 17–3 heading into the fourth quarter. That's when the Rams came alive. St. Louis scored two touchdowns and tied the game with 1:37 left. With no timeouts left, Brady drove the Patriots 53 yards down the field to set up a potential game-winning field goal. Kicker Adam Vinatieri nailed a 48-yard attempt as time expired, and the Patriots were Super Bowl champions for the first time in team history.

At 24 years old, Brady was the youngest quarterback to win a Super Bowl. He also earned the Super Bowl MVP

Award for his performance. It seemed like a Hollywood ending to an unbelievable underdog story. But the story was only just beginning.

DOMINANT DYNASTY

Brady and the Patriots didn't stay underdogs for long. After finishing 9–7 and missing the playoffs in 2002, Brady led the Pats to a 14–2 record in 2003. They made it to Super Bowl XXXVIII against the Carolina Panthers. Brady and the Patriots' offense shined in the championship game. Brady threw for 354 yards and

Brady holds up the Super Bowl XXXVIII trophy in February 2004. He also earned his second MVP Award in the victory over the Carolina Panthers.

three touchdowns. But it still wasn't enough to shake Carolina. In another tense finish, the teams combined for 37 fourth-quarter points. Brady appeared to put New England up for good with just under three minutes remaining. Patriots linebacker Mike Vrabel lined up as a tight end for a trick play. Brady threw Vrabel a 1-yard touchdown pass, and New England led 29-22.

But the Panthers answered back with a quick touchdown drive to tie the game. There was 1:08 left when Brady took over again. He drove the offense 37 yards in a hurry. Vinatieri once again hit a last-second field goal. The Patriots were champions again, and Brady won another Super Bowl MVP Award.

The Patriots began the 2004 season 6–0, giving them 21 wins in a row. That was the longest win streak in NFL history at the time. They went back to the Super Bowl after two dominant playoff wins. Brady threw two touchdowns in a 24–21 win over the Philadelphia Eagles. Over a four-year span, Brady and the Patriots won 57 regular and postseason games and three Super Bowls, cementing the team as a dynasty.

FAST FACT

Brady threw two touchdown passes in the Patriots' 41–27 victory over the Pittsburgh Steelers in the 2004 AFC Championship. What made that even more impressive is that he had spent the night before fighting a 103-degree fever.

Chapter Three

NEARLY PERFECT

The New England Patriots continued to roll after winning Super Bowl XXXIX. Brady led the team to a 12–4 record in 2006. The Patriots looked to be headed back to the Super Bowl. Early in the AFC Championship game, they led the Indianapolis Colts 21–3. But Peyton Manning led a comeback to an eventual 38–34 Colts victory. The matchup deepened the rivalry between the sport's two best quarterbacks.

The loss made the Patriots a motivated team heading into the 2007 season. And Brady was teamed up with another superstar. Wide receiver Randy Moss had been one of the league's best pass catchers for a decade. But the 30-year-old had never been to the Super Bowl.

Moss quickly became Brady's favorite target. In their first game together, Moss had nine catches for 183 yards and

Brady looks to pass during the 2006 AFC Championship Game against the rival Indianapolis Colts.

a touchdown. That success continued all season. The Patriots had the highest-scoring offense in NFL history. And New England also rolled up wins. The Patriots entered the final week of the regular season 15–0.

Brady's final touchdown pass of the season went to Moss in a 38–35 win over the New York Giants. It was Brady's 50th passing touchdown, breaking Manning's previous single-season record of 49 for most in a season. More importantly, it helped clinch a perfect regular season for the Patriots, as they became the first team to finish 16–0. On top of that, Brady earned his first league MVP Award.

Hall of Fame receiver Randy Moss, *right*, teamed up with Brady in 2007 to form a potent combination.

In 1972 the Miami Dolphins had finished the regular season undefeated and won the Super Bowl. No team had done it since. But in that era the NFL played only 14 games during the regular season. When the Dolphins clinched perfection, they were 17–0. The 2007 Patriots entered Super Bowl XLII with an 18–0 record and a chance at history.

Waiting for Brady and New England were the Giants again. Led by Eli Manning, Peyton's younger brother, New York shocked the heavily favored Patriots. The Giants held Brady to 266 yards passing and a single touchdown. New York pulled out a late 17–14 victory. New England's perfect season was over.

COMEBACK KID

Coming off an undefeated regular season, the Patriots were favored to win the Super Bowl in the 2008 season. But their season was derailed in the first quarter of the first game. A Kansas City Chiefs defender hit Brady in the knee, resulting in a season-ending injury.

Brady recovered in time for the 2009 season. Once he was

FAST FACT

Tom Brady and Peyton Manning formed the NFL's best quarterback rivalry throughout the 2000s. Manning retired in 2015 with five MVP Awards to Brady's three. But Brady won 11 of the 17 head-to-head matchups between the pair, and in the 2020 season he won his seventh Super Bowl while Manning had just two.

FAST FACT

A superstar on the field, Brady has also gotten a lot of attention for his personal life. Early in his career he dated the actress Bridget Moynahan, and they even had a son together. However, his celebrity really exploded when he began dating supermodel Gisele Bündchen. They married in 2009 and later had a son and a daughter together. But in 2022, the couple announced they were getting a divorce.

on the field, Brady played like his old self. He threw for over 4,000 yards and was named the NFL Comeback Player of the Year. In 2010 he led the league in touchdown passes and was named the league MVP again. But in both seasons, the Patriots lost their opening playoff game.

Playoff success returned after the 2011 season. Brady threw six touchdowns in a 45–10 victory over the Denver Broncos in the divisional round. Then the Patriots dramatically beat the Baltimore Ravens 23–20 to reach another Super Bowl. They hadn't played in one since losing to the Giants four years earlier. Super Bowl XLVI was a rematch between the two teams. The Patriots were favored to win once again. But Eli Manning led another upset.

By 2014 the Patriots had put together 11 straight years of at least 10 victories. But New England had not won the Super Bowl since 2004. Even at 37 years old, Brady was still one of the league's best quarterbacks. He threw for 4,109 yards and 33 touchdowns as New England finished 12–4.

Brady drops back to pass during Super Bowl XLVI against the New York Giants. The Patriots lost 21–17.

The Patriots routed the Colts 45–7 to reach the Super Bowl again. Brady threw three touchdown passes in the AFC title game win. That matched New England up with the Seattle Seahawks in Super Bowl XLIX. Facing a tough Seattle defense nicknamed "the Legion of Boom," the Patriots fell behind 24–14 at the start of the fourth quarter. Brady then rallied New England back. He closed the gap to 24–21 on a touchdown pass with 7:55 left. New England quickly got the ball back. Brady completed all nine of his pass attempts on a 10-play, 64-yard drive. With 2:02 left he capped it off on a three-yard scoring play to receiver Julian Edelman. New England now led 28–24.

The Patriots defense intercepted a pass at the goal line in the final seconds to seal the win and put the New England dynasty back on top. Brady was named the game's MVP for the third time.

Controversy followed the victory. The Colts accused Brady and the Patriots of deflating footballs in the cold weather for the AFC title game. Balls with less air pressure would be easier for Brady to grip. The league did indeed find that the balls Brady threw in that game had not been inflated to the proper level. The scandal, known as "Deflategate," dragged on all summer. Brady was initially suspended for his role. However, that suspension was overturned just before the start of the 2015 season. Brady didn't miss a game and led the NFL with 36 touchdown passes.

He also led the Patriots back to the conference championship game. There, he came up against Peyton Manning one final time. Now with the Denver Broncos, Manning won the defensive duel, 20–18. Denver went on to win the Super Bowl. It was the 39-year-old Manning's last season. But Brady would be back again.

Tom Brady holds up the game ball after beating the Baltimore Ravens 35–31 in a divisional playoff game on January 10, 2015.

Chapter Four

THE G.O.A.T.

Winning Super Bowl XLIX gave Tom Brady his fourth championship. That tied him with Joe Montana and Terry Bradshaw for the most Super Bowl championships won by a quarterback. Montana was widely considered to be the greatest quarterback in NFL history. Brady put himself into that conversation with his fourth Super Bowl Championship win.

The 2016 Patriots compiled a 14–2 record and cruised into Super Bowl LI after two dominant playoff wins. Waiting for them were the Atlanta Falcons. The Falcons had a potent offense led by quarterback Matt Ryan, who won the league MVP Award that season. And that offense was on full display in the Super Bowl. Midway through the third quarter, Ryan threw a touchdown to put the Falcons up 28–3. No team had ever come back to win a Super Bowl when down by more

Tom Brady reacts to the New England Patriots' 28–24 victory over the Seattle Seahawks in Super Bowl XLIX.

FAST FACT

Tom Brady and the New England Patriots made a lot of Super Bowl history. Super Bowl LI was no exception. It marked the biggest comeback in Super Bowl history. It was also the first Super Bowl to go to overtime.

than 10 points. Brady would have to make more history if he was going to win his fifth title.

Brady responded by leading four scoring drives. That included marching the offense down the field in overtime. That drive ended with running back James White scoring to give the Patriots an improbable 34–28 win. Brady won his fourth Super Bowl MVP Award after throwing for 466 yards, the most in Super Bowl history. And after a fifth championship, there was not much debate left over who was the NFL's greatest player ever.

Brady came back even better in 2017. He led the league in passing yards and won his third league MVP Award. And the Patriots made the Super Bowl again. Brady broke his own record for most passing yards in a Super Bowl when he threw for 505 yards and three touchdowns. But it wasn't enough, as the Pats lost to the Philadelphia Eagles 41–33.

The Patriots bounced back in 2018 and once again made the Super Bowl. Just as in Brady's first Super Bowl in February 2002, the Pats faced the Los Angeles Rams, who had moved from St. Louis five years earlier. Brady didn't get the headlines this time, as the New England defense held the Rams the entire game to secure a

Brady looks to pass against the New York Jets during the 2018 season.

13–3 win. That win made Brady the only player in NFL history to win six championships.

NO END IN SIGHT

Brady and Patriots head coach Bill Belichick had achieved historic success together. However, many noticed their relationship was deteriorating. Brady often disagreed with Belichick's decisions, including on how to build the roster. Belichick was also known as a tough coach who was famously demanding of his players.

FAST FACT

The Patriots made the Super Bowl three years in a row from 2016 to 2018. They were the first team to play in three consecutive Super Bowls since the Buffalo Bills reached four straight championships from 1990 to 1993.

Before the 2020 season, Brady decided to move on. He left New England with fond memories and wrote a letter to fans stating how he felt. In it, he said, "You opened your heart to me, and I opened my heart to you. And Pats nation will always be a part of me."

Brady signed with the Tampa Bay Buccaneers. In a new, more laid-back atmosphere, he was reenergized alongside his old friend Rob Gronkowski. After a slow start to the 2020 season, Brady and the Buccaneers won their final four regular season games. They then went 4–0 in the playoffs. The streak was capped off by Brady's historic Super Bowl touchdown pass to Gronkowski against the Kansas City Chiefs. That score propelled Tampa Bay to a 31–9 victory. Brady threw for 201 yards and three scores while clinching his seventh title. His legacy was secure. However, Brady returned in 2021 and led the NFL in passing yards and touchdowns at age 44. After the Buccaneers lost in the divisional playoffs, Brady announced his retirement. But it didn't last. In March 2022 Brady announced he was returning to Tampa Bay.

Brady spent one more season with the Buccaneers, leading them to the playoffs again. In November 2022 he became the first NFL quarterback to surpass 100,000 career passing yards. After Tampa Bay lost in the wild card round, Brady announced his retirement. He said this time it was for good. For one of the greatest quarterbacks to ever live, there was finally nothing left to accomplish.

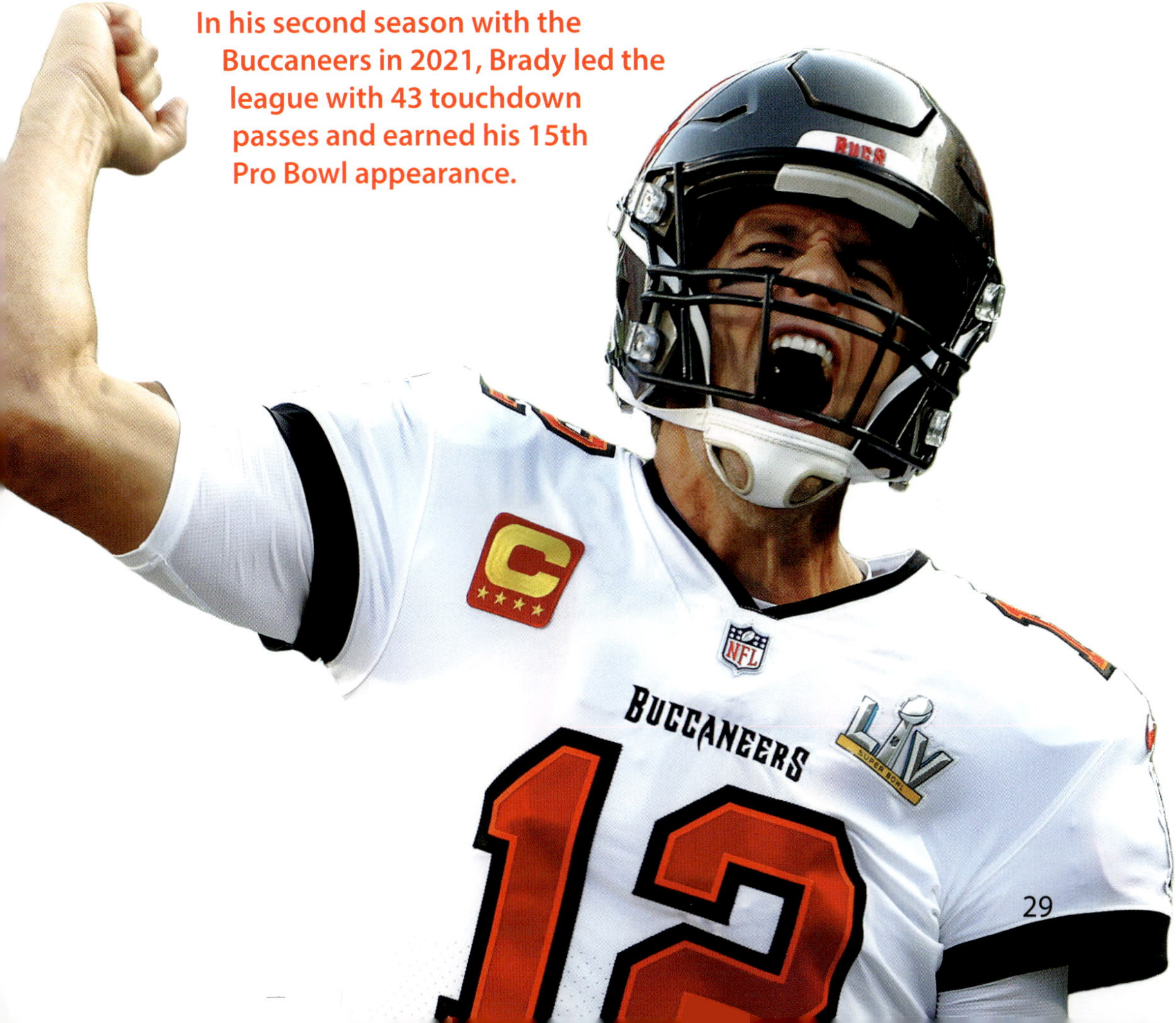

In his second season with the Buccaneers in 2021, Brady led the league with 43 touchdown passes and earned his 15th Pro Bowl appearance.

GLOSSARY

contract
An agreement to play for a certain team.

depth chart
A sheet that shows starting players and their backups at each position.

draft
A system that allows teams to acquire new players coming into a league.

dynasty
A team that has an extended period of success, usually winning multiple championships in the process.

end zone
The areas at each end of a football field where teams try to score touchdowns.

rookie
A professional athlete in his or her first year of competition.

scholarship
Money awarded to a student to pay for education expenses.

shotgun
A formation in which the quarterback lines up five to seven behind the center and takes the snap in the air.

underdog
The person or team that is not expected to win.

MORE INFORMATION

BOOKS

Abdo, Kenny. *Tom Brady*. Minneapolis, MN: Abdo Publishing, 2022.

Buckley Jr., James. *Who Is Tom Brady?* New York: Penguin Workshop, 2021.

Graves, Will. *GOATs of Football.* Minneapolis, MN: Abdo Publishing, 2022.

ONLINE RESOURCES

Booklinks
NONFICTION NETWORK
FREE! ONLINE NONFICTION RESOURCES

To learn more about Tom Brady, please visit **abdobooklinks.com** or scan this QR code. These links are routinely monitored and updated to provide the most current information available.

INDEX

ABOUT THE AUTHOR

Luke Hanlon is a sportswriter and editor based in Minneapolis.